Messages

on

Dried Leaves

Yolanda T. Marshall

Garnalma Press
Publisher@Garnalmapress.com
Ontario, Canada
www.Garnalma.com

ISBN: 0995310335
ISBN-13: 9780995310339

GARNALMA Press

To the adventurous souls who fell in love with Poets

CONTENTS

ACKNOWLEDGMENTS

Messages on Dried Leaves is a mild resurrection of my first poetry book, *Obayifo*. This book is a collection of personal notes, texts, emails and voicemails sent to muses of the past.
Special thanks to Raymond A. Anderson, an amazing Poet/Author, for granting me permission to use a couple of his masterpieces. This Garnalma Press publication is exactly as I intended it to be and I am thrilled to share it with my readers. To my Graphic Designer N. Khan, I requested a simple cover page and you made it happen. To all the people who insisted that I release a second book of poetry, I hope you enjoy and I am grateful for all your support. Of course, to the souls who bravely fell in love with this Poet, you inspired me. Cheers!

Remember when dinner dates served us butterflies?
The first time you stared into my eyes
So many words I wish I had said
So many times, I regretted it to this very day
You were wrong and I was too young
As dried leaves infuse in my cup of tea
I wonder if you think of me

Having you reassures, I am no longer lost
Three simple words at the end of each day leads me
out of chaos
"I Miss You"

You don't know the parts of your body I have touched
The fantasies on my poetic mind would make you blush
I want to sit with you on the sands of Jamaica
Cool the heat of our bodies in Negril's water
Drink, talk and eat in the vast of laughter
Stare into your eyes – that lucid glass ball of my future

.

Kissed you with my smile
sigh
Why?
My lips were too far away
from your beautiful skin

Every kiss is a sip of euphoria
Exchanging vibrations of sweet Karma
Access to touch your aroused skin
A blessing to gratify such sin
Thankful for the energy we share
I appreciate having you near

Your touch made me forget of the fools I once entertained
Your strength held me up high, when I thought I was failing
Life… if life offered such abundance every day, I would rather be rich with you in my pockets
My eyes have never and will never wonder, my kisses are yours to keep
I will host private parties; you will be the only guest
Let us celebrate your attendance

I enjoyed you, under the night's skies,
While the moon kissed the river
Revealing your bright smile, like reflections upon
darken water
My hand gliding softly across your lips
Just to trace its definition with my soft fingertips
Bliss!

One look at you and my knees gravitate to the floor
How can I complain when your eyes and smile
open countless doors?
Into a life of flaws and adornments – simply
human
Unpredictable, progressions appreciated, on a path
close to perfection

Sweet silence... beautiful silence
The scent of passion rises from this moment
Mother Earth paused for a second, my body
breathes
Exhales all waste, all woes, all that it does not
need
Inhales the presence of your masculinity
Kissing flow effortlessly
In this moment, souls realize
Life at its best exhumes ~ comfort

My body felt secure in your comforting hands
Waking up to a new day, gifted with divinity
A new sun, setting a new moon
A new me, with you

What we have is real, we feel this in good or bad, weak or strong
I love cooking as tunes play and you mischievously play with me
Love exploring and exploiting a few, new possibilities
Love burying my face in the depth of your chest, close to your heart
Love the way I feel now, at my best, knowing you were mine from the very start

I am here, where I should be
Away from my past of emotional injuries
I can breathe, I can feel, I can live in this
newfound paradise
You are my home, a sacred place – in your life

Gazed at your profile photo on many occasions
Mentally electing you to save me from complicated
relations
Rescue my heart from that 'fuckboy' who calls
himself a man
Respect me, love me, the way I should be and only
you can
Comfort me, after I walk away from him

When my pen strokes the paper
my mind wanders
and every word I write
creates the sight
of you

I never believed size mattered
Until I rode your rollercoaster
Screaming to get off, yet my adrenalin craved more
More, more pain with pleasure
You measure thicker and longer
Than any other brother
That hook

Bonded by unspoken emotions
Even in the presence of distance, keeping us
physically apart
This is not a coincidence or a rabbit tail fortune
This is us, we, you and I exposed to dimensions

If you were to cry, my eyes will shed tears,
accompanying yours, defining togetherness
If your heart were to break, sleepless nights will
find me picking up all the pieces

How do you like your women, your flings or flirts?
what attracts you to them, their eyes or skirts?
Who do you allow to feel your swollen member?
where do you touch them, how many do you
remember?

How can I enter your world of lust and love?
What can you offer me, other than the moon and
sky above?
Who do I have to be, to gain possession of your
heart?
Where can I find you and when can we start?

Baby, this is so awakening
I am always smiling
while we are texting
visualizing you and I kissing
touching
moaning
grinding
fucking
your voice has me yearning
for that wake-up call every morning

The words you said
Still lingers in my head
Come to think of it
The tone of your voice
Melts me, like heat to ice
Causing my nipples to rise
Crafting rivers between my thighs
Wow!
Baby, you make me
Weak in the knees

Mmmmm ... I can taste your skin
A drink of brown Chocolate Sin
I'm tipsy
Erotically
Ending a dispirited day

Hey, let's get away
from the drama, we face everyday
glance into my eyes
as you slither your fingers between my thighs
feel me
stir me
absorb my wetness
as you descend into my sweetness

You, black like an endless tattoo, an African son
Teeth white like
Skin smooth like
Lips plumped like
Eyes deep like
Bones strong like
Body toned like
Tall like
Smell good like
God planted fresh flowers
To bloom and heal my heart forever
Perfected to my taste
Like… you escaped Babylon's waste

I was up for an adventure, obviously — you opened the doors to that possibility
I walked in freely… knowing you might not be right for me

You left me recovering from pleasurable pain, to resume positions over and over again
I felt you, dancing to fit it in and pacing not to get it out

Your eyes pierced my brain, this is insane
Your name creates freestyle, repeating a classic
rhythm
Fires burn in the speed of movements as our bodies
played on B-flat, deeper and deeper

*I want you to be my protector, my best friend, and
my rock when all feels gloom
I will be your strength, your organs of pleasure and
a heart with endless room.*

Strong minds abiding, respecting, supporting,
Communicating, compromising, aging and
preserving
Living with this, this is -
Love

Your happiness pours joy into my life, it uplifts all
beliefs I have in you
There is no home for grudges here, just breaths of
truth in the air

I am satisfied with your modest gestures,
blossoming my uncontrollable smile
Infectious you have become
Like candy for my inner child

I can see myself dedicating my life and love to you
Pledging to the laws of loyalty, praying for this
union to be blessed from the spirits above

Let's do it again, while crickets are singing in the
bushes
Making it hard to hear my muffled moans
Our eyes locked into the deepest stare
Cold winds tickled our skin
As warm organs played in sin
Blanketed by the moon
In the park

Poetry is waking up to you every morning
If this is living poetry, in desirable strophes
I will never need a pen again

You spoke, in a language new to me, yet I understood
Ulinipenda… lakini walikuwa uhaba

Your smile, a sibilant chorus
Your lines, your notes make my heart skip beats
In rhymes, rhythms of intelligence echoes
Drums assimilate into the base of my heart,
Beating an addictive song ingrained in my flesh

Tonight, let's role play
I will be feeding your needs
Accepting your seeds
Mmmmm
Under a scantily clad costume,
You will find me, the one you adore
Your whore

If my mind captivates you
traps, stimulates and intrigues you
love it for what it is and enjoy it
for our inner abilities are unlimited, a perfect fit
love it, protect it, possess it, demand it

Mailbox
I knew that I could never love you like the ink
loves the page.
And yet I also knew that I couldn't force my heart
to remain in this lane, but I did.

I am without excuses or without lies to cover my
tracks.
Or possess any bandages to cease the leakage from
your eyes.
But this time I knew that your heart is truly
broken.
And I can't begin to find the focal point to explain
why my heart carries symphonies for another.

Maybe it's because when I called you I never fully
felt engaged.
Or maybe when we kissed I've never felt teenaged.
But I've never been one to read to caution labels
on products.

In fairness, there are fragments of my heart left on
your front porch.
I once breathed the same air you exhaled out.
At one time, we were once each other's fabric and
we simply torn apart at the seams.

Like dried leaves on my window sill, our time
together is up. - -Raymond A. Anderson

You aren't real
Your words played a game
I accepted those lines
Like a glass of expensive wine
Intoxicating my mind
I refuse to waste anymore of my time with you

"I often forget to tell them I love them
Just as often as I forget to show them."

-Raymond A. Anderson

I cannot recall when last you sent a compliment my way
Muted, I have been whimpering from night to day

I am trying to remind you of what resides in me
Staying close, hoping the softness of my skin
Will make you beg to re-visit my body
Just when I build up all the strength to make you
want me
Many moons passed, outshining my beauty
One, you've never seen

*If jealousy allows me
to judge immaturely
exposing my possessive nature
of needing to be your only lover
then it shall become my failure*

Look at me
Can you see what I see?
A shivering demon
An uncultivated woman
She haunts me in my sleep
And laughs when I weep

When I lack sympathy
I will forget the feeling of pain
I'll get aroused as my daggers rain
Just when you think I am bruised
I will delete all feelings for you

I do not want to let you go
Even though I know
You represent the strength of insanity

I was your hope
Your dreams of me were vacations where you
eloped

I want what you have – that map to greener
pastures of romance with another lover
You can take back your seeds of unhappiness
Let them grow envious trees in your soul

Did I not keep up with you?
Didn't I remain strong?
Should I have strayed and betrayed you?
Like you have done to me?
Humiliated me?

I am bitter because you made me this way when you opted for the wrong paths...was led astray

I cried by my window last night
After we endured that brutal fight
Unable to control my turmoiled life, wishing death
on you, I cried

A part of me died
Perfect lovers they claimed we are, perfect home
Perfect passion between us they believed
There should be no need to roam
Yet, here I am, angry, pacing all alone

Darkness is overshadowing my light
Played my guitar, creating a place where love and
attraction ignite
An ideal world, where we never fight
My fingers strummed vivid images of sweet
harmony
Trying to drown out the sound of your feet
walking away from me

I am trying to manage this heartbreak, playing sad love songs
But every powerful song bellows high and low notes; reminding me that it is what it is and always will be
A tragedy
Unwillingly, I drift out of my aesthetic sound clouds to face reality

I still love you, yet I must accept the end
They will say I left, because you were too old
But the truth is, I am too young
There is so much more I want to experience
Please let me go

It is over for real this time
Stop calling my phone
One thought of your presence seduces me to accept
your propositions
Now here I am again
I keep coming back to cum like rain

*You couldn't distinguish between the sounds of
our names
You thought you would play the honest role
Trying to be what you are not
Faithful*

Let go of my hand
Free me from your web of deception

That path I missed a few steps before I entered your hell, I found it

To my melancholy past I lost sight
Au revoir pain
Life's too short to be withdrawn from love, from
self-respect
There are risks to take and a soul to protect
So, I moved on

I don't miss you, which was simple to do
It is so easy to forget 4 inches, when I am buried
6 inches deep, under a thick layer of erotic ecstasy

You said I am not the woman you knew
I agree with you
The woman in my mirror is different than the one I
was used to seeing
Every time I look at her, she applies an expensive
lipstick and vows to never kiss weak men like you
Ever again...

Written on my branches, worn like sleeves
Love came, Love shared and Love lost
I stand with my head held high as a tree
Sheading old, bitter-sweet messages on dried leaves

Yolanda T. Marshall

ABOUT THE AUTHOR

Yolanda T. Marshall is a cross-genre writer/Poet.

www.ytmarshall.com